If You Don't Fit In,
STAND OUT!!

Insights, Reminders and Affirmations

by

Warren Hay Lyons

Copyright © 2001 by Warren Lyons
Revised January 2006

All rights reserved. No part of this book shall be reproduced or transmitted in any form or by any means, electronic, mechanical, magnetic, photographic including photocopying, recording or by any information storage and retrieval system, without prior written permission of the publisher. No patent liability is assumed with respect to the use of the information contained herein. Although every precaution has been taken in the preparation of this book, the publisher and author assume no responsibility for errors or omissions. Neither is any liability assumed for damages resulting from the use of the information contained herein.

ISBN 978-0-7414-3156-1

®WGA 820799
Library of Congress 2001

Published by:

INFI∞ITY
PUBLISHING.COM

1094 New DeHaven Street, Suite 100
West Conshohocken, PA 19428-2713
Info@buybooksontheweb.com
www.buybooksontheweb.com
Toll-free (877) BUY BOOK
Local Phone (610) 941-9999
Fax (610) 941-9959

Printed in the United States of America
Published May 2013

Many friends have given me encouragement to write *and publish* this book. Especial thanks to:

Barbara Hayes, Benjamin Lyons, Betty Ann Solinger, Don Weiss, Ernest Lehman, Jacqueline Joseph, Jean Franzblau, Jeff Bridges, John Scaringi, Judy Lyons, Karl Wood, Lee Stickler, Marcia Seligson, Mark Bryan, Paul Livadary, Richard Hefner, Sharon Sharth, Steve Ross, Tom Bresnahan, and Va. Lloyd.

This book was edited by Lee Stickler

For Tootsie
Who makes me happy when skies are gray

For Pal, Sister, and Little Warren
Remembrance of Cats Passed

Author's Explanation

All my life, I wanted to fit in, and for many years I did - in my family and in New York. Then a play I co-produced, John Guare's trail-blazing black comedy *The House of Blue Leaves*, won the New York Drama Critics Circle Prize as "Best American Play," and I fell into a maelstrom of confusion, a seemingly-bottomless pit of pain.

My life did not make sense. Emotionally, I had prepared myself for failure, for a life of no worth. Yet here I was - a success.

I moved away and began to assess my purpose and my talents. First, my purpose: to bring joy to myself and others. I had to learn to include myself. I was born in the heart of Broadway and for thirty-one years, I was entranced by the opening nights, champagne, telegrams, famous faces and names, maitre d's, velvet ropes, penthouses, parties and restaurants. Somewhere along the way, amidst the excitement, distraction and unimaginable upward mobility, I got lost.

It wasn't easy to find my path and stay on it. You want easy? Order in. Want peace of mind? Ah, me, then the game's afoot. Once the door of insight opens, it won't be closed. I hope these insights, ideas and suggestions spur you and speed you to the magic combo of peace, prosperity and productivity.

Warren Hay Lyons
January 26, 2006

Introduction

I participated in Warren Lyons' *Joy of Singing!*™ workshop way back in 1979. In fact, I learned so much about life and relationships that I did it twice in a row - first by myself and then with my wife. I discovered that the "muscle" that lifts us up into the act of singing is the same one that opens up *all* our creativity.

In *If You Don't Fit In, STAND OUT!!*, Warren has given us powerful tools and ideas, based on his *Joy of Singing!*™ guidelines, that cut to the core of his philosophy which inspires and enables us to be peaceful and productive.

After twenty-five years, I continue to be a pitchman for Warren and *Joy of Singing!*™ and I recommend the workshop all the time.

Jeff Bridges
January, 2006

If You Don't Fit In,
STAND OUT!!

e on time.
It's an excellent way
to show respect
for the order of God's Universe.

B

**Nobody is
"Fine, thank you"
all the time.**

Not even you!

Isn't that a relief?!?

Now you can relax and be yourself!

**All you can do
is all you can do.**

**So *please:*
BE KIND TO YOURSELF!**

Be yourself.

Do the best you can.

Allow yourself the only constant life offers -

C-H-A-N-G-E .

If what you are doing does not work,
do something else!

Power is the ability to do or act.
To win, *use your power*
when you think you don't have it,
and especially
when you are *sure* you don't have it.

Trust,

Take action,

Let go of the need to control.

When you walk through a storm, *take a friend!*

Ask for what you want
and be aware of
expectations.
They keep us from being in the
present,
where God is,
and pave the way for disappointments.

Please:
No cheap jokes
or sarcastic remarks
at anyone's expense -
and especially
not your own.

They are too expensive!

Don't go where *you know* You are *not* wanted.

Criticism without balancing praise can destroy or harm.

Always follow words of criticism with praise.

WORRY

and dis-satisfaction
accomplish
nothing,
and aren't even fun!
They have only one value:

MOTIVATION
TO
ACTION

Take nothing and nobody for granted.

*Nothing lasts forever –
not happiness, not grief.
Even Cats, the musical, closed.*

*Only God,
the Source of Our Selves,
is eternal.
So be grateful
for what you've got
while you've got it!*

Trust God, Thank God!

Transformation has five stages:

1. Be where you are

2. Follow your instincts

3. Take chances

4. Deliver the goods

5. Accept appreciation

Appreciate yourself and others,
and *accept appreciation*.
Feeling deserving of appreciation
- joining your fan club -
may be the most difficult thing
you do,
and the most rewarding.

Compassion
has two elements:
forgiveness and appreciation.

Can you forgive and appreciate
those you love or have loved
and yourself?

It requires practice, eh what?

It will be
whatever
it will be:
whatever
God has in store
for me.

*Let Go
and Let God
lead the way.*

Imitate God.
God does not punish.
God teaches.
God does not judge.
God accepts.
Imitate God.

If you imagine the worst,
envision the best.

"I am" is a process.
"I'm not" is a habit.

If you have nothing to say,
don't say it!

Take your place!
Foreground pays better
than background.
Stars earn more than extras.
Do what it takes to come
out of hiding.
Take your place!

Talents are natural abilities.
Use 'em or lose 'em.
And if you suffer
the "Curse of the Multi-Talented,"
use one talent at a time!

Patience is the Eternal Lesson,
always practiced,
never mastered.

Practice Patience!

Get where you're going, *then* eat.
This avoids mad-dashing,
and helps digestion.

If you don't know
what you want,
be grateful
for what you have.

If you have boxed yourself in, look for the way out!

HAVE NO NEW REGRETS.
THE OLD ONES
ARE HEAVY ENOUGH,
THANK YOU VERY MUCH!
AND, ESPECIALLY,
No graveside regrets!

HOW MUCH
HAPPINESS
CAN YOU TAKE?

HOW MUCH
PLEASURE?

ARE YOU SURE?

Practice the
principles that lead to
peace and productivity.

Which principles?
You decide.
But practice 'em!

What always feels good:

OVERCOMING THE ODDS!

Don't wait 'til I'm dead
to tell me you love me.

The secret of happiness:
Balance.

Surrender: what has happened,
has happened
Take action: do something
- or nothing!
Trust: have faith in yourself,
God and other human beings.

Do you know how

WONDERFUL

you are?

If not, there is work to be done,
to be done!

Don't expect anyone to love
or appreciate you
if you don't!

It won't sink in.

The presence of emotional, psychic
P-A-I-N
suggests there are lessons to be learned, mistakes to be corrected.

Q. #1
How much of our lives is spent
in wasted anxiety,
dreading the worst,
and expecting disasters
that never occur?

A. Too much!

Our American habit:
wasted anxiety
Our American problem:
too much choice
Our American way of sharing:
selling

THE LOST INGREDIENT IN OUR SOCIETY:

Silence.

Feeling *worthless*?
It's just a feeling.
It will pass.
Everything passes.
The dinosaurs roam no more.

What is God?
God is perfection.
God is life.
Then life must be perfection.

Why don't we see it that way?
Habit, attitude,
mis-perception.

NO DEPRIVATION
ALLOWED!
It serveth nobody!

Our walls are walls of

F-E-A-R.

Our greatest fear? The unknown!
Boogie-boogie!!

Parents can not –
and ought not –
protect their children forever
from pain, disappointment
and loss.

These are inevitable.
Far better to *prepare* them.

Practice
the Art
of
Attraction!
Brush your hair,
smile if you feel like it,
and do the next thing before you.

Repeat after me
"I will not be
treated as an after-thought!"

Stay open!
Stay in motion!

Q. #2
Is it possible to dig from the present
back to buried and long-denied feelings
of loss, rage, and disconnection,
to be restored to love and joy?

A. They put a man on the moon,
didn't they?

Q. #3
The path to maturity may include
massive blocks of fear
and negative energy.
You built them and they appear strong.
Are they?

There is more PAIN in denial
than in acceptance.
In fact, there is no PAIN in acceptance!
It's on the path from denial
to acceptance
that sometimes we experience
all that PAIN.

That's why so many of us don't even set
foot on the internal journey.
It demands great courage and is fraught
with *feelings*.

There are worse combinations
than
some money,
lots of ideas
and great potential.

E-X-P-A-N-D
or
contract.

Them's the choices.

Is it alright with you
not to be *nice*?

Love requires no work;
relationships, however, do.

To see yourself as a success, focus on any area of your life in which you do not criticize or judge yourself.

Any.

In that area lies the first step of growth.

THE ROAD OF LIFE HAS BUMPS.
THIS DOES NOT MEAN
THAT YOU ARE AT FAULT
OR
THAT YOU HAVE CHOSEN
THE WRONG PATH,
VEHICLE OR PARTNER.

IT'S JUST THAT
THESE THINGS HAPPEN.

To have and enjoy a successful life, we must heal ourselves by eliminating blame and shame, and focusing on forgiveness and gratitude. This is different from manual labor. It's *spiritual* labor, the kind our parents never warned us lay ahead. Why not? *'Cause they didn't know about it!*

What some call
a "nervous breakdown"
may actually be
a healthy opportunity
to arrange your priorities,
re-examine your choices,
and clear your vision.
It might even be the rising
of murk that has lain dormant
for too long,
and a sign of corrective action that
is growth.

When there is nothing to do,
do nothing.
Sometimes this is more difficult
than doing something.

Q. #4
How many of these insights, reminders and affirmations are you practicing?

A.

WHAT ARE YOU DOING NOW to be HAPPY?

If you don't fit in,
STAND OUT!!

About the Author

Warren Hay Lyons is the second of four sons of New York Post columnist Leonard Lyons and his witty wife, Sylvia. It was a family in which dinner companions included Marc Chagall, Joe DiMaggio and Ethel Merman.

Raised by a workaholic father and a compulsively critical mother, Warren naturally became a work-addicted self-critic. To his dismay, he found that no professional success - including acting in two Broadway comedies, working for producer David Merrick on twenty-one Broadway shows, winning the prestigious New York Drama Critics Circle Prize for his original co-production of *The House of Blue Leaves*, writing for the front page of the New York Times Arts and Leisure Section, manager of Talent Development at ABC TV, and co-producing *Lyrics by Ira Gershwin*, which starred Frank Sinatra, Liza Minnelli, Tony Bennett and Bernadette Peters at the Dorothy Chandler Pavilion - none of this stopped the insatiable, wagging finger of perpetual self-condemnation.

Only when he played the piano and sang, did the racket stop. So that's what he did: played and sang professionally until one day the work dried up and the blanket of criticism returned full force. Warren knew he had to sing *or die*, and became passionate about claiming his birthright: the freedom to communicate without fear and self-criticism. In the summer of 1977, painfully and spontaneously, he combined his search for peace of mind with his theatrical experience and love of music and founded the *Joy of Singing!*™ in his Manhattan living room. Two years later, Warren moved it to his new home in California, and has produced and/or directed more than 230 three-day *Joy of Singing!*™ workshops on both coasts. Past students include Jeff Bridges, Marianne Williamson, Rue McClanahan, Mark Bryan and Michael Feinstein.

Warren wrote and performed his one-man show, *My Life in 'The Lyons Den,'* from 1993 until 1998, when he was diagnosed with Parkinson's Disease, which is not contagious, and which he views as the latest in a long list of stimulating challenges to a joyful life. His next book is a true memoir of his life.

To contact Mr. Lyons, or for more information about *Joy of Singing!*™ write to:

warrenlyons@juno.com

Made in the USA
Columbia, SC
23 December 2020